MANAGER MANTRAS

Volume 2

Great Manager Institute

ISBN 978-1-64828-091-7

Contents

Introduction by Editor

Great Manager Institute was born with a vision to create a world where every individual gets an opportunity to work with a Great People Manager. We aim at identifying the real differentiators of Great People Managers - their managerial practices.

While a single formula for learning people management may not necessarily exist, because every individual is unique and every organization is different, a single powerful pattern that we have observed across 5000+ surveyed managers is that the best people managers work on a small number, but consistent practices that ultimately lead to remarkable results. The journey of becoming a Great People Manager is continuous, with a series of small wins and everyday progress.

We believe that all the managerial practices proceed through three pillars of people management - Connect, Develop, Inspire© and through this book, we have classified the mantras adopted by India's Top 100 Great People Managers using this framework. These mantras have helped these People Managers fulfil their potential, and we are sure you'd like to fulfil yours too.

We credit all the mantras to the winners of Great People Manager Study 2019, conducted in association with Forbes India.

Preface

Leveraging your people managers to produce great business results

- Prasenjit Bhattacharya

Most organizations have a vision and mission and a social purpose with employees who are inspired to give their personal best. Right?

Wrong!

For most organizations and their promoters, the business of business is to make money. Reality is that you need customers, talented employees, good relations with the government, suppliers and other stakeholders to make money.

If you are working in such an organization, your owner or employer will seek to understand how any intervention aimed at creating high engagement for employees will make more money for the organization. This is a great question because this positions creating high employee engagement along with other business initiatives to make more money for the business.

We have numerous examples of making more money by creating great engagement. For this article, let me use an example from the banking industry.

While designing a great people manager intervention that has a direct link on tangible results, we broadly followed the following steps.

The first step is to understand how robust the business model is. People familiar with what is happening in the banking industry will know that technology and disintermediation is changing the structure of this industry dramatically. There is a strong possibility that the traditional business model may change significantly and any change will impact people.

Why is this understanding important? The design of the intervention will be different if we are expecting major disruptions in the business model in the next five years. In this case, while the changes are being perceived, the bank did not anticipate a major impact on their people in the next five years. This gave us the opportunity to show some quick business results.

We looked at the option of working with the senior leadership and quickly abandoned the idea - the credibility of the leadership team was fairly high (based on our customised employee survey feedback), and while many things they do directly impact the goal of making money, very few of these directly impact the day to day experiences of the employee.

The obvious target group was line managers- branch heads in consumer banking and middle managers in other lines of businesses- managers who have teams of people reporting to them. We call them people managers.

Why would busy line managers, already struggling with customer issues, now take additional accountability for such an intervention? To answer this question, we asked the line managers that if we were to design an intervention to help them with their three most important goals as managers who manage teams, what would be those three goals. Their responses can be clubbed into three categories: The intervention should

1. Help us achieve our business goals
2. Get my people to give their personal best
3. Support my team in collaborating with each other with minimal involvement from me

They had one strong criterion. It should not increase their work load!

How can a manager achieve all the above three goals, create a great workplace culture, and yet not increase her work load? The answer to this question led us to re-discover what great people managers have always done. They have focussed on the quality of their interactions rather than on the quantity, using each interaction as an opportunity to build more trust. Our research, and those of many others, has shown that higher levels of trust co-relates with better business results, higher individual performance and better teamwork.

Research done by The Great Manager Institute, showed that great people managers did not just do different things, they do even the same things *differently*. It was the way of doing a meeting, celebrating success, or even doing a performance appraisal - they had unique ways of interacting with their colleagues that enhanced the quality of interaction and increased the level of trust. All of them were able to do three things well- Connect with their team members, Develop them to realise their potential and Inspire them to give their best. (CDI)

How do we get line managers with different levels of people skills to do the above? We took them in batches of 25 for two days to a workshop to help them to understand the following:

1. Managers regardless of personality and personal styles can build trusting relationships.
2. Many managers are already doing so. In survey after survey, in multiple organizations, we find that there are managers whose teams feel that their immediate workgroup is a great place to work. If all managers had teams whose perceptions were similar to theirs, the organization would be a great workplace.
3. You can create a great workplace experience for your team regardless of how average the overall organization is. A manager can create a great workplace experience even if corporate policies are not helpful.
4. Data shows a direct link between creating a great employee experience and better business results.

The managers who went through this program were given practical tools to understand how they can convert day to day interactions as opportunities to build trust - a way of working that makes day to day work less like transactions and more like sharing of gifts.

We introduced three levels of certification. Level 1 certification was when the manager goes back to his manager and his team to share his plan. Level 2 is when the manager is able to share at least two success stories (or learning stories even if not a success) in a peer to peer platform created for managers going through this program. Level 3 was when an independent third party survey of their team members could establish that the team members have seen a perceptible difference in pre-defined behaviours that lead to greater trust.

This came to be known as the people manager certification program. To make sure that the program is perceived to be rigorous, a minimum 20 per cent improvement as perceived by team members was a pre-requisite to certification.

About 70 per cent of the managers could achieve level 3 certification in 4 months' time. What does this changed behaviour in branch heads in a period of 4 months mean for the business? Even as we completed the first batch we saw that the managers who could complete all three levels of certification showed better results in parameters such as current and savings account deposits, fixed deposits, retail assets, net interest income, cost-income ratio and attrition.

That is the time when the business heads started to take notice. Now this is an organization-wide program for all people managers with two clear objectives - improve productivity and reduce attrition.

If the business of business is to make money your great workplace intervention should directly impact making more money.

In this booklet, we have compiled simple practical practices of real line managers who have been recognised as some of the best people managers by Great Manager Institute. They are not specialists. Like most of us, they have targets that they achieve through their teams. The difference between them and many others is that they have realised that building a better quality of experience for their team members is the only sustainable way to build the business.

Happy Reading!

Prasenjit Bhattacharya is a Director at Great Manager Institute. Views expressed are personal. You can post your comments and join the discussion in Prasenjit's blog on Linked in. Prasenjit can also be contacted at
prasenjit.bhattacharya@greatmanagerinstitute.com

CONNECT

A Great People Manager connects with
his/her team by communicating regularly
and clearly, caring for them, seeking
feedback and being fair.

Mantra: **Presentation by new hires**

- *Manoj Naik, Nexval Infotech Pvt Ltd*

He organizes presentation sessions by new hires, where they present on a topic of their choice. He believes that this initiative enables them to connect well with their new team and gives them ample opportunity to lay down the golden growth chart for each of them.

Mantra: **Born to Lead**

- *Nagarajan S, Mahindra & Mahindra Financial Services Limited*

Every month, the team member who performs exceptionally well, is given a chance to serve as a leader for the rest of the team. The newly elected leader can propose new ideas and lead initiatives for the team. Nagarajan S, as the people manager shares information and guides the new elect, whenever s/he needs assistance.

Mantra: **Deciding the level of intervention required**

> - *Tarapada Sahu, Feedback Energy Distribution Company Ltd*

Certain tasks need to be micromanaged while some need to be macromanaged. As a people manager, he, in discussion with the team, decide the same at the onset of the task. As a result, team members have clarity about whether they need to report hourly, daily or on completion of the task. His mantra gives people the clarity while eliminating the discomfort arising out of micromanagement.

Mantra: **Using different strokes for different folks**

> - *Vidyasagar Moningi, Kelly Services India Pvt Ltd*

According to him, each team member is at a different development level and comes from a different background. As a people manager, he identifies whether a particular team member is new in town or is battling a personal issue or if any other developmental or environmental barrier is preventing him/her from giving their best. He then creates solutions to resolve his team members' problems being it helping them make travel arrangements, or allowing them to work from home.

Mantra: **Hamara ICU**

- *Dr. Reshma Tewari, Artemis Hospitals*

Dr. Reshma believes in making her medical team feel like one cohesive unit. To put this in practice, she has created a Whatsapp group where they can communicate openly. In this group, team members post about their requirement of a sudden day-off, and it particularly makes a difference since they continuously handle medical emergencies. As a result of this, team members step in for their colleagues during times of illness or personal difficulties. This practice has helped relieve stress and create a positive, transparent environment.

Mantra: **15-minute rule**

- *Arif Khan, Rakuten India Enterprise Pvt Ltd*

As part of a daily Huddle, he organizes a simple 15-minute get-together, just talking about 3 things that each one is working on, the progress and the hurdles. If someone is stuck on a problem, other team members pitch in to help. This fosters teamwork and an open culture of not being judged or embarrassed to ask for help.

Mantra: **Know your team**

- *Amit Ramani, Awfis*

With his support, his team has developed an app that carries the details of all the team members (name, photo, qualifications, and tenure at the organization). Through this, the team has been able to know their team members well and personalize interactions with each other. This mantra has particularly helped new employees at Awfis, feel welcome.

Mantra: **Bonding as a friend**

- *Krishan Kumar Gautam, EdCIL (India) Limited*

He ensures that he bonds with his team members as a friend and not as a boss. To achieve this he has regular casual conversations with the team and introduces humor in conversations to keep the mood light.

Mantra: **Storytelling**

> - *Shalil Gupta, News Corp Mosaic Media Ventures Pvt Ltd*

As a manager, he motivates his team members to share stories around their wins at work, at regular intervals. He believes that this is the best way of recognizing risk takers and those who take up new challenges.

Many managers routinely post such stories in their Intranet to encourage their team member and others.

Mantra: **Cross-functional collaboration**

> - *Dr Arun Balakrishnan, Omniactive Health Technologies Ltd*

To ensure alignment between R&D and marketing teams, he organizes brainstorming sessions between the two teams right from Day 1. This helps in increasing the pace of product development, eliminating the silos and establishing a common vision. His mantra has a unique stamp of people management and collaboration.

Mantra: **Organizing Town-Halls**

> - *Deepak Shrivastava, Amway India Enterprises Pvt Ltd*

To enable collaboration amongst team members, he has ushered in the concept of a 'Town Hall' every week, wherein everyone gets an idea about what the department is doing, priorities for the upcoming times and contribution of every team member to the department as a whole. The "town hall" lasts for an hour. It brings in transparency and allows everyone to share their ideas publicly.

Mantra: **Pass on**

> - *Sunil Vishwakarma, Dream11 Fantasy Pvt Ltd*

With a belief that knowledge should be shared and not hoarded, he has a weekly catch-up where all the team members share and guide their peers over the knowledge they've acquired over the week. Knowledge sharers are further appreciated through a small treat.

Mantra: **CEO & COO Interaction**

> - *Venkat Sujit Samrat Chintakindi, Broadcast Audience Research Council India*

He ensures that the team members interact with the CEO & COO of the organization every quarter, helping them showcase their learnings to the senior management - while the senior management understands the perception of people concerning the vision, strategies that the company has adopted.

Mantra: **One Team, One Goal**

> - *Siddhartha Srivastava, PNB Housing Finance Ltd*

To ensure that the team is aligned towards a common goal, he keeps himself updated on the micro and macro issues in the organization - and updates his team on the same.

Mantra: **Scavenger Hunt for Onboarding**

> - *Ramana Prasad Kovelamudi, Prasad Hospitals India Pvt Ltd*

To add a fun element to the conventional onboarding process, he has developed an innovative 'scavenger hunt onboarding process'. He turns information that is usually considered boring into company trivia and makes the new joiners find answers to them.

Mantra: **Scheduling regular one on ones**

> - *Murali Krishna Gannamani, Fluentgrid Limited*

He schedules one on ones with his direct reports every alternate day to ensure that all his team members are on the same page. This reduces redundancy and helps his direct reports feel that he always has their back.

Mantra: **Ditching the formalities**

> - *Manan Lahoty, previously associated with L & L Partners, now with Indus Law*

To encourage people to manage time better and make them feel comfortable, Mr. Lahoty has eliminated the formalities in internal communication for juniors. For instance, he introduced a mantra where juniors can write a short email in the subject line itself, thereby eliminating the pressure of writing good emails.

Mantra: **Microblogging**

> - *Gaurav Seth, BENO SOFTWARE*

To resolve issues that developers face, he has created a microblogging platform in the organization, where developers can write their problems and tag their respective managers, who then know that there's an issue that they need to look into. This has helped him achieve two things - instant problem solving and increased satisfaction level of developers.

Mantra: **Quick breaks**

- *Santhosh Shyamsundar, Aditi Staffing India Pvt Ltd*

He takes at least one break daily with his team members to ensure bonding outside office space. Apart from this, he plans weekend get-togethers to engage with his team after work.

Mantra: **Mentoring from within**

- *Simarneet Wahi, HDFC Life Insurance Ltd*

Rather than hiring external coaches for mentoring, she identifies members within the team who can hand-hold the rest of the team through the difficulties that they face. This ensures that there's a comfort level and the team members can share their issues openly.

Mantra: **Humor at work**

- *Jayesh Joshi, Nexval Infotech Pvt Ltd*

While juggling a wide range of management roles, he uses a unique mantra of breaking barriers through humor. Be it team meetings, one-on-ones or town hall meetings, he believes that a leader with a great sense of humor creates positivity and helps the entire team loosen up - opening the communication line from top to bottom.

Mantra: **Know your team**

- *Gurjodhpal Singh, PayU Payments Pvt Ltd*

As a people manager, he spends time with every new hire in the team, to understand their family background, hobbies and aspirations. This helps him in engaging with his team in a meaningful way, and makes the new employee feel valued.

Mantra: **Daily huddle for a collaborative leadership**

- *Dr. Shikha Tiwari, T. John College*

Having 15-minute huddles to ensure that the required stream of information moves through the organization periodically and systematically, is her mantra for connecting with her team. Her daily stand-ups aim at an instant resolution of issues, thereby creating a comfortable workspace ambience.

Mantra: **Let's talk**

- *Dr. Ankita Singh, CIGNEX Datamatics Pvt Ltd*

To build trust and encourage candid communication, she arranges an open meeting every quarter, where all the team members discuss their issues openly with complete transparency. She has created a rule that if any team member has an issue with somebody from the team, they can voice it openly during the meeting, rather than indulging in any whispers later.

Mantra: **Speaking Helps**

- *Tejasa Purandare, Cosign India Pvt Ltd*

She conducts regular monthly interactions to help the team members understand their performance - actual versus expectation. It's a casual interaction wherein they discuss what is missing at both the ends, and the steps that the team, as well she as a people manager, could take to improve their performance.

Mantra: **Speak your heart out**

- *Brijesh Singh, Fast-Track diagnostics Asia*

Speak your heart out is an initiative where all the team members can discuss their expectations from the leader and their vision for the organization. This helps maintain transparency and keeps the management updated on what is happening at the ground level.

Mantra: **Walk-the-talk**

- *Debasis Panda, Avnet India Pvt Ltd*

A practice that he has been following for more than a decade, his mantra is to have a 5-minute chat with every team member daily - where he simply listens to his team members & provides a solution to their issues. He ensures that he continues this practice even when he is out on a tour by connecting with his team members over a phone call.

Mantra: **Conducting stay interviews**

- *Kevin Freitas, Dream11 Fantasy Pvt Ltd*

His team members' opinions matter to him and to hear them out he conducts "Stay Interviews" every six months. In these interviews, he puts forth the following questions:

- What do you wish to learn?

- What do you think while coming to work?

- What makes you stay with us?

Mantra: **Driving new initiatives**

- *Nitin Sharma, Raychem RPG Pvt Ltd*

He spends time with every team member to come up with new initiatives and helps them plan the same in detail. Then a review is undertaken for every action item identified by them. The team that completes the intended initiative as planned, is rewarded every quarter.

Mantra: **Two Truths, One Lie**

- *Dharmendra Jain, YASH Technologies Pvt Ltd*

As a people manager, he understands that sometimes it's hard to meet deadlines or fulfill unreasonable demands made by clients Thus, before the start of every monthly team meeting, his mantra is to have every member tell two truths and a lie that they told during the month, to attain client satisfaction. What they have is 15-20 minutes of eyebrow-raising, thought-provoking introspection and laughter as they look back at what it took to get the job done.

Mantra: **A token of gratitude**

- *Anshul Jain, Cushman & Wakefield India Pvt Ltd*

Every New Year's Day, he sends a personal, handwritten note to the spouses and children of his direct reportees. Through this, he thanks them for their continuous, year-round support that enables his team to deliver their best every day.

Mantra: **Caring for every individual**

- *Virendra D Sanghavi, Aarvi Encon Limited*

Besides his role as a leader, he also considers himself responsible for his team's safety. To ensure workplace safety, Mr. Sanghavi organizes workplace safety trainings that impart his workforce the knowledge and skills to perform their work in a way that is safe for them and their colleagues.

Mantra: **Managing deadlines**

- *Suketu Modi, Smarten Spaces*

He believes in being updated about the progress of the team, particularly in projects with steep deadlines, thereby making them feel that they have the support and can come up to him in times of difficulties. He also offers them additional support by arranging transportation, if the employee is staying back late at work.

Mantra: **Life is beautiful post 6.30 p.m.**

- *Ankur Shah, HDFC Life Insurance Limited*

His constant endeavor has been building a culture of mutual respect and managing a healthy work-life balance across teams. He evaluated the activities happening towards the end of the day and categorized them into Do's, Don'ts and Non-Value Adds. Taking a step ahead, he laid down business rules for cut-off times for Meetings, conference calls and reviews to institutionalize his mantra.

DEVELOP

A Great People Manager develops his/her team by providing and seeking constructive feedback while providing growth opportunities

Mantra: **Empowering**

- *Sunil Takale, Omniactive Health Technologies Ltd*

For any new assignment, he lets his team members take initiative and execute their ideas - unless there are major diversions in the workflow. It makes them feel empowered and boosts their morale. He has been following this practice since the past four years and it has helped his team members grow a lot.

Mantra: **Zero tolerance culture**

- *Himanshu Kumar Chauhan, Hella India Lighting Ltd*

To cultivate a zero-tolerance culture towards customer dissatisfaction, team members generating customer delight are awarded a Green Card, while team members causing a delay in a task are given a Yellow Card. His practice has been very effective in both motivating and raising an early alarm in case of delays.

Mantra: **Gratitude Tennis**

- *Paul Breloff, Shortlist*

With "gratitude tennis", he has introduced a practice where two people "volley" notes of appreciation/gratitude about a third person back and forth rapid-fire. This inspires trust and helps people understand the value of their work. It also creates a positive environment, knowing that others see you in a good light.

Mantra: **Organizing hackathons**

- *Hari Charan Rao, Rakuten India Enterprise Pvt Ltd*

As a manager who always imbibes the culture of innovation, Mr. Rao organizes a hackathon wherein teams come up with prototypes and proofs-of-concept for new projects. It serves the purpose of getting newer ideas and creating a bond amongst folks who further work towards a common goal. This mantra has helped the team propose newer projects in multiple departments and gain Management's appreciation.

Mantra: **Boss for a day**

- *Rajesh Kumar Bhoi, Feedback Energy Distribution Company Limited*

Juniors often wonder what their bosses do all day. To address this, he gives his juniors a chance to be the 'boss for a day'. He believes that this mantra gives the juniors a taste of what it's like to be in charge and changes their attitude. He believes that understanding what one's boss does, can help one perform better at his/her own job, while appreciating theirs.

Mantra: **Who will take my seat?**

- *Shailesh Kalrao, Feedback Energy Distribution Company Ltd*

He encourages team members to share a part of his responsibility. If they handle the responsibility successfully, he hands over the entire portfolio to them, while granting them a promotion. This helps both in building capabilities and in creating a leadership pipeline.

Mantra: **Adopting newer technologies**

- *Mustufa Batterywala, Impetus Infotech India Pvt Ltd*

To make sure that team members acquire new skills, he encourages them to get enrolled for tech initiatives outside the scope of work. This helps the team members get practical exposure, while allowing the organization to reuse their newly acquired skills in projects.

Mantra: **Shark Tank**

- *Arun M Vijayan, Beroe Consulting India Pvt Ltd*

When there's a need for an 'out of the box thinking', Mr. Vijayan conducts a 'Shark Tank' where he brings in a 'War room' exercise. In this exercise, the team member may suggest ideas for completing the project that are discussed, questioned and deliberated by the rest of the team, and the best idea wins a 'Kudos' card.

Mantra: **Fortnightly coaching**

- *Manoj Pramanik, Cinepolis India Pvt Ltd*

As a manager he undertakes fortnightly visits to every unit. He observes the best practices of the unit and identifies practices that need improvement. Post every visit, he shares his suggestions with the team, which makes them feel both motivated and guided.

Mantra: **Encourage, Empower**

- *Shveta Mahajan, Cushman & Wakefield India Pvt Ltd*

She consciously empowers all her team members by letting them interact with clients directly, encouraging them to lead newer growth areas and placing them in situations of authority early on.

Mantra: **Job enrichment**

- *Shantanu Das, Amway India Enterprises Pvt Ltd*

As a manager, he lets his team members take up additional projects apart from their core roles. These could be as diverse as change management or talent acquisition - at both national and global levels. Through this, the team is able to gain a diverse experience and a deeper understanding of business.

Mantra: **A book per month**

- *Neeraj Chauhan, PayU Payments Pvt Ltd*

What initially started as a 'Daily 10 minute Reading' session, has now become a thumb rule wherein his team members have to complete at least one book every month. It could be a comic, a magazine or any non-fiction book. Through this, he tries to broaden the thinking of his team members.

Mantra: **Leveraging untapped potential**

- *Mini Sharma, BSI Group India Pvt Ltd*

She has created an avenue of learning and enhancing income by encouraging the administrative staff to do telesales. Over a period of two years, her team members were able to double their salary and the organization benefitted through additional sales - a win-win for both.

Mantra: **Understanding strengths and weaknesses**

- *Parixit Ashar, ACG*

He believes in identifying the strengths and weaknesses of his team members and allotting tasks accordingly. He also works on converting weaknesses into strengths. For instance, when he identified that his back office team was weak in MS-Excel, he arranged a special training for them.

Mantra: **Research tracks**

- *Vivek Gupta, Impetus Infotech India Pvt Ltd*

He plans regular research tracks within his team, promoting Cagle competitions, Hackathons, and other online competitions to enhance the combined knowledge of the team. This also includes sending teammates to various events on data science across different locations.

Mantra: **Being HR Plus**

- *Shuchi Nijhawan, Eka Software Solutions*

Every team member has a job enrichment duty along with their usual KRAs. She therefore encourages all the team members to contribute outside of the HR function to other teams, be it design, marketing, program management or other functions. This helps them get an even deeper understanding of the business and provide relevant solutions to the business problems.

Mantra: **Constant improvement**

> - *Abhishek Kulkarni, Property Solutions India Pvt Ltd*

Through this mantra, he maps the team members for annual training only after conducting a 1:1 with them. This helps him understand the team members' expectations and train them accordingly.

Mantra: **Go Back-2-Basics**

> - *Ravinder Rana, Concentrix Daksh Services India Pvt Ltd*

With his Back-2-Basics initiative, Mr. Rana ensures that all the team leads, managers and account heads have a defined checklist that they follow while connecting with people. His intelligent people practice ensures that his team knows how to coach and engage people. Following the success of this 'Manager Mantra' in India, it has been replicated globally too.

Mantra: **Higher involvement**

- *Naveen V, Apollo Hospitals*

As a manager, Naveen ensures that he goes on the field with his field representatives, to strengthen the relationship with referral doctors and be there for his team members whenever they need support. This ensures that he understands the crux of the business, and is involved at the ground level with his team.

Mantra: **Why-Why**

- *Kalyan Kadam, Shree Ashtavinayak Glass Pvt Ltd*

As a manager, his mantra is to make his team think. So if his team member is stuck at a point, he avoids providing the solution directly. In such cases, he calls for a brainstorming session, where he places the question "why", and does not provide the solution until the team is close to the answer.

Mantra: **Bottoms up approach**

- *Partho Dasgupta, Broadcast Audience Research Council India*

He ensures that every management trainee presents suggestions and improvements to the senior management, on completion of their stint in the respective department. This helps in bringing in newer ideas from early entrants, and giving them exposure early on.

Mantra: **Knowledge sharing**

- *Vikram Singh Bopche, Hafele India Pvt Ltd*

He always makes it a point to share upcoming developments with reference to any field with his team, thereby keeping them updated on what's happening around. This could be as diverse as data analytics, or their own field.

Mantra: **Let me help you**

-   *Ravi Kumar C, Nexval Infotech Pvt Ltd*

He conducts a daily huddle to discuss the team strategies and deliverables lined up. This huddle helps him understand concerns or issues that need his immediate attention.

Mantra: **Maker's time**

-   *Navaneethakrishnan R, HackerEarth Technologies Pvt Ltd*

With a belief that context switches are expensive in the engineering world, he has adopted the 'Maker's Time' philosophy, wherein all the 1:1s are planned after 5 p.m. This ensures that everyone has a low context switch during their work hours & the team has observed a 30% rise in productivity post this.

Mantra: **Gift-a-book**

- *Satish Sundaresan, Elektrobit India Pvt Ltd*

To help a team member or a peer navigate through their personal or professional challenges, he gifts them a book tailored to their needs and the nature of the challenge. His gesture has helped several team members grow mentally, psychologically & emotionally.

Mantra: **Individual attention & support**

- *Sridhar Siripragada, Property Solutions India Pvt Ltd*

He believes in giving individual attention to his team members' challenges, queries and conflicts, if any. This helps in developing clarity and improving productivity.

Mantra: **PEP Talk**

- *Rashmi Ranjan Patra, Omniactive Health Technologies Ltd*

His mantra is to constantly motivate his team members through a PEP talk, where he shares his experiences on different subjects and makes the team understand the 'how' and 'why' of performing a particular activity and its importance. By applying this mantra, his team has begun taking ownership at work and has started influencing other team members to deliver.

Mantra: **Job chat**

- *Prarit Aggarwal, Mahindra Holidays & Resorts India Ltd*

Job Chat is a manager mantra through which he understands the aspirations of the team members that could be related to their professional life, such as wanting a promotion or a salary increase, or personal goals. He conducts an informal chat with his team members before their appraisal, and creates an environment that would facilitate achievement of these aspirations. This mantra has made him a sought-after mentor in his team.

Mantra: **Personal Development and Career Goals**

- *Ganesan S, Biesse Manufacturing Co Pvt Ltd*

Apart from discussing the individual and departmental goals, he takes time out to discuss the personal development and career goals of every team member, at least once a month. After understanding their aspirations, he helps them understand how they can achieve the same and offers specific guidance.

Mantra: **Who wants to be the Unit Head?**

- *Roshan Sinha, Cinepolis India Pvt Ltd*

He conducts a role play for a day wherein his reportees get an opportunity to get into the shoes of a Unit Head and perform the tasks of a Unit Head for a day. It gives the team a chance to understand the skills and thought processes required to lead, thereby inspiring them to do better.

Mantra: **Design Sessions**

- *Manish Sharma, dunnhumby*

He organizes a design session wherein developers volunteer to work on new designs and once the designs are prepared, they are presented to the team. The team as a whole discusses all the options available along with the pros and cons of each. This mantra maintains transparency and gives every developer an opportunity to take ownership. Through this, he has developed a new line of leadership for his team.

Mantra: **Career progression talks**

- *Rajdeep Mandal, Mahindra & Mahindra Financial Services Limited*

The majority of the people managers avoid having career progression talks with their teams. However, Rajdeep considers such quarterly talks as an opportunity to identify future leaders and groom his team members for the future. He helps them understand how they should think, act and behave for being considered as the next choice for leadership roles.

Mantra: **Change of role**

- *Krishnan Kalyanaraman, Ozone Group*

With a belief that monotony kills productivity, he gives his team a chance to handle different areas such as documentation, banking, corporate compliance, and litigation to break the monotony. His initiative makes his team members feel that there is something for them to learn daily and they look forward to taking up newer challenges.

Mantra: **Be the boss**

- *Rashmi Sharma Mankad, Hafele India Pvt Ltd*

She asks her team to lead the project - whether it is presenting the business case to the management during a monthly meeting or sending a critical piece of communication to everyone across the company. Before every such meeting, she conducts a role-play to help her team members prepare better and build their confidence.

Mantra: **Make-my-job-redundant**

- *Sudheer Bandaru, Shortlist*

He encourages team members to make him redundant in every possible way. For example, he tells his team members, "You don't need me on the next big deployment or client meeting? Great, thank you, I am around in case you need help!"

He adopts this mantra for almost every reversible task. His practice has helped develop self-managing teams, thereby helping them gain confidence - giving him the time to strategize and innovate.

Mantra: **Switch**

- *Dilipkumar Khandelwal,*
  Previously associated with SAP India Pvt Ltd

Switch is a job rotation program that he runs in his team. It enables his team members to switch the jobs and responsibilities with a person who is not from the same team or function. The 3 week assignment enables his team members to be very agile and take up assignments on a short notice.

INSPIRE

A Great People Manager inspires his/her
team to give their personal best by
recognizing their contributions and
celebrating together

Mantra: **Innovative chef of the week**

> - *Tanay Goregaonkar, Yellow Tie Hospitality Management*

Every week, he tells all the Chefs to create a new dish - with both a unique name and a unique taste. He limits the number of ingredients that can be used to 6 and keeps a budgetary limit to get the best from less. The best innovator of the week is awarded a crown that s/he can wear. The Chef maintaining the crown for a month is awarded the "King of Innovation" certificate. The dish which the innovator innovates is put on the revised menu and the name of the chef is printed in the "Golden Book" of the organization.

Mantra: **Creating opportunities for all**

> - *Raghunath Jonnavithula, Manoj Vaibhav Gems N Jewellers Pvt Ltd (Vaibhav Jewellers)*

As a people manager, he identifies the unique qualities of his team members and helps them scale up their ability to take up newer challenges. For instance, when he observed an office boy working on images on his office computer, he encouraged him to learn Photoshop. After letting him to create layouts, today the 'office boy' has grown to be an 'Assistant Manager' and designs creatives for their organization.

Mantra: **One small step**

-   *Rohan Bhansali, Gozoop Online Pvt Ltd*

Every week he organizes an initiative - an act of kindness that Gozoopers can be a part of and take "one small step" towards helping the society. He, along with his team members, have pioneered several activities including a T-shirt painting event at an orphanage and an event involving preparation, distribution of 1,000 sandwiches to the needy.

Mantra: **Evangelism Drive**

-   *Mukesh Sharma, QA InfoTech Software Services Worldwide*

With a belief that knowledge should be shared, he encourages his team members to participate in conferences and workshops. He also organizes internal conferences, where the winners and strong contenders are awarded a prize for presenting well.

Mantra: **Set it on fire (Aag Laga Do)**

- *Raj Jha, Mahindra & Mahindra Financial Services Limited*

To motivate Sales Executives, he organizes a one-day competition (annually) amongst them wherein they have to achieve the maximum targets on that day & 'set the sales on fire' basis a list provided to them. This mantra helps create a positive environment and reduces complacency in the sales team.

Mantra: **Up skilling**

- *Aikta Tyagi, Amway India Enterprises Pvt Ltd*

As a manager, she ensures that every team member completes at least two skill-based pieces of training annually as per the need of their job role. She believes that this practice keeps them updated on the global trends and gives a momentum to their career.

Mantra: **Always there to pick you up**

- *Sriram T, Cushman & Wakefield India Pvt Ltd*

He makes it a point to take his team members for a coffee or lunch whenever they lose a big deal. This cheers them up and makes them feel that he is there to lift them up when they fail.

Mantra: **Create and share**

- *Harshal Ichale, Gozoop Online Pvt Ltd*

Whenever they get a new project, he encourages all the team members to come up with a unique solution, and the best one is selected. The team member who suggests the best solution is appreciated and gets to work on the project.

Mantra: **Q Cube**

- *Faiyaz Engineer, ACG*

Q CUBE stands for Quality, Quality, Quality (QQQ). As a manager, he undertakes a one-on-one quality talk to drive quality consciousness into the minds of the team. His objective is that when his team members think about the product being developed, they should be sensitive towards it being perfect.

Mantra: **Think big**

- *Asheesh Joshi, Signify Innovations India Ltd*

As a people manager, his mantra is showing his team the larger picture of doing a project well and making them understand the impact a project would have on their growth. He encourages his team to take educated risks for chartering new areas and stands by them in case they err in the process.

Mantra: **Confidence building activity**

-   *Peeyush Shukla, Casa Brands India Pvt Ltd*

His mantra is to assign a task that is one level-up from his team members' existing duties. He believes that this boosts their confidence and he monitors the performance continuously, to ensure that if anything goes wrong, they would have support.

Mantra: **See the big picture**

-   *Bansi Raja, Gozoop Online Pvt Ltd*

Her mantra is to look for the bigger picture in everything that they do, as a team. She believes that being aware of the larger canvas and understanding how one's work adds value to the larger scheme of things, instills a higher level of accountability. While assigning a task to anyone in her team, she walks them through why they were chosen for this task, what skill they possess that would be needed to accomplish the task and how things would look when they accomplish the task - helping them place themselves in the bigger picture.

Mantra: **Identifying and nurturing HIPOS**

- *Gagan Jyot, RMSI Pvt Ltd*

She identifies HIPOS (High potential) team members through a series of assessments including aptitude assessment and behavioral profiling. Post that, she creates strategic leadership development plans for the HIPOS to enable them to grow to leadership roles in the organization. This sets a benchmark and inspires other team members to up their game.

Mantra: **Devil's advocate meetings**

- *Malligeswari Panneerselvam, Beroe Consulting India Pvt Ltd*

She has introduced this innovative mantra for key pilot reports. In this exercise, the analyst from her team presents their work to the rest of the team. And the team then takes the role of a Devil's Advocate where the key objective is to raise doubts and challenge the analysis made thus far. This ensures that there are no loopholes in the report and that the analyst has thought through all the options that can be implemented in the report.

Mantra: **Recognition through 'Bravo Blue Darter Awards'**

- *Anil Khanna, Blue Dart Express Ltd.*
  (Now associated with Vakrangee Ltd)

In his past role at Blue Dart Express Ltd, he ushered in a practice of giving an on-the-spot reward to his team members for any extra-ordinary efforts that they had taken during the course of day-to-day work. The award entitled the awardees to a Commendation Certificate signed by him, a Bravo Blue Darter Memento and a cheque of Rs. 500/-.

Mantra: **Saying 'Thank You'**

- *Kinchit Shah, Ami Lifesciences Pvt Ltd*

Whenever his team member completes a task within timelines by implementing a new idea or thinking out-of-the-box, he makes it a point to say 'Thank You' to the team member. The practice of saying thank you, which is very obvious but highly underused, makes the team member feel invaluable and motivated

Mantra: **Recognizing champs**

- *Miguel Munoz, Mahindra Holidays & Resorts India Ltd*

He recognizes every employee with a special talent (for instance, dancing or singing) as a 'Champ'. Champs are facilitated with work time for practicing dancing or singing. They can then perform in front of guests visiting the resort. As a result of this, employees with a special talent are able to further develop their skill, and there is an immense value addition in the customer experience.

Mantra: **Achievement log book & handwritten appreciation cards**

- *Nikulkumar Panchal, ACG*

He maintains an 'Appreciation Diary' wherein every team accomplishment is logged. He also notes the tasks that need improvement and provides feedback to the team members needing improvement. He gives a handwritten 'Appreciation Card' to members going over and above the call of duty, along with appreciation in front of the entire team during the daily huddle.

Mantra: **Involving budding leaders in the annual planning cycle**

    -   *Prasad Guntupalli, Attra*

He conducts an annual planning session every year where he also invites the high potential performers with leadership potential (who are not directly a part of the management team) to participate and get a ring side view of how the company is functioning. This mantra is appreciated by the team members as it prepares them for a larger role.

Mantra: **Thought leadership initiatives**

    -   *Harish Soundararajan, Beroe Consulting India Pvt Ltd*

If he feels that a team member has performed exceptionally well, he recommends his/her work to the organizational marketing team - that uses the insights to publish blogs or to conduct webinars. This is a quarterly activity acting as a great platform to help the team members gain recognition from external stakeholders, helping them make their work visible to the world.

Mantra: **Winning Wednesdays**

- *Ranjan Banerjee, Crowne Plaza Today New Delhi Okhla*

As a manager, he has ushered in a practice of "Winning Wednesdays", wherein he celebrates the weekly wins of his team members through 'Thank You' Cards. Winning practices include doing the right thing, showing that they care, aiming higher, celebrating the difference, and collaborating well.

Mantra: **Appreciating best practices**

- *Surojit Phukan, Signify Innovations India Ltd*

He appreciates the best performer of the month and his/her best practices in monthly team meetings. This makes them feel appreciated and recognized. For instance, when a team member surpassed the expected performance level, he appreciated him and the team member was treated to lunch.

Mantra: **Smile Please**

Ashima Roona, Cinepolis India Pvt Ltd

Every week she sets up a meeting which is known as the 'Priority meeting'. Here she divides the yearly goals into small weekly goals and over a period of time measures the progress of the same. Team members who complete 100% of their assigned priorities get a smiley badge that can be displayed on their desk. The team member who accumulates the highest number of badges at the end gets a special award - for instance, a compensatory off.

Mantra: **Appreciation**

- *Alok Pratap Singh, CORE Diagnostics Pvt Ltd*

He recognizes the best performer of the team and shares their best practices with other team members. This helps them identify gaps in their own performance and up their game.

Mantra: **Pay it forward**

- *Payal Sinha, dunnhumby*

For appreciating the work done by her team members, she writes an appreciation mail marking her seniors and gives the top performer a reward card, known as "Pay it Forward". This boosts the morale of the top performers and motivates other team members to keep striving to reach greater heights.

Mantra: **Living My #LifeAtIHG**

- *Rishabh Tandon, Crowne Plaza Today New Delhi Okhla*

His mantra involves sharing stories of colleagues who went above and beyond the call of their duties. These team members are appreciated through the Facebook Page of IHG, which has a reach of more than 45,000 fans. Team members love being recognized on social media, and it has served as a motivator to his millennial team members in particular.

Mantra: **Retention Premier League (RPL)**

- *Sayan Bandyopadhyay, HDFC Life Insurance Ltd*

He has launched a quarterly contest within the team for retention where he rewards the top 3 winners with a certificate, based on a fixed set of parameters. This has developed a connection between him and the team members along with harboring a sense of pride amongst the winners, thereby containing attrition.

Mantra: **Nurturing creative minds**

- *Sonica Gurung, Aditi Staffing India Pvt Ltd*

To enable risk-taking amongst employees and to help them think creatively, every month the most creative team member gets a 'Star of the Month' award, prepared by the rest of the team - including personalized pictures and handwritten notes.

Mantra: **Creative corner**

- *Rajarshi Debray, Signify Innovations India Ltd*

Everyone is encouraged to share something creative weekly, which could be a piece of self-curated music, photos, drawings, blogs, travelogues or even movie reviews. His idea is to help people appreciate life beyond office hours that goes a long way in improving the quality of life.

Mantra: **Khushi ki Ghanti**

- *Shubha Goel, The Akshaya Patra Foundation*

Khushi Ki Ghanti or Ring the Bell is a mantra introduced to applaud instantly and celebrate every win at work. To recognize people, she has created a mantra that whenever a target is achieved or a team member has his/her anniversary, their manager rings the floor-bell, and the employees have to applaud the announcement made.

BONUS MANTRAS

Some mantras adopted by managers from great workplaces

Mantra: **Rumor has it**

To address rumors/ water cooler discussions openly and transparently, a leader places a bowl in the common area where team members can drop rumors they are hearing. In the monthly meeting, the manager reads and addresses these rumors to create a culture of openness.

Mantra: **Echo box**

An "ECHO BOX" is placed in the department for the team to drop their ideas, concerns, wishes and issues. The team members can keep themselves anonymous while putting in their ideas and suggestions. All the ideas, concerns, wishes or issues are collected and discussed in the Monthly team meeting for a possible resolution. The objective of this mantra is to gain inputs from all team members who might otherwise be hesitant to share their thoughts.

Mantra: **Apna Junction**

The team meets fortnightly to reflect on the positive and negative things at work. Although driven by managers, the managers themselves aren't involved in this meeting. This ensures that the team can discuss freely and share their thoughts on what's working and what's not.

Mantra: **Golden Values**

With an objective is to inspire team members to work towards the organizational goals and values, people managers organize the 'Golden Values' event on the last Friday of every month. Here the poster with 'Company Values and Priorities' is pasted in the meeting room and one value is chosen. Teams ensure that the chosen value is reinforced in all conversations with the customers and internal stakeholders.

Mantra: **Pathshala - Gyan ka sagar**

Aimed at employees' career development, these are a series of knowledge sharing sessions within the teams where every week employees choose a particular topic and discuss the same. Effectiveness of the session are measured by defining the KPIs. These sessions ensure involvement of the team members, team bonding by being empathetic to everyone's views.

Mantra: **Lessons Learnt**

The people manager creates a database called "LL (Lessons Learnt)" where employees upload significant lessons that they've learnt while working on different projects. Nukkad groups of 3-4 employees are made on rotation basis where these lessons are presented and discussed.

Mantra: **Main bhi dekhu (Let me see)**

The idea is to develop skills and competencies of the team members and expose them to different roles. The people manager divides the team into pairs and lets them understand each other's work in detail. This practice helps a team member appreciate their peers and turns out to be a great boon when a member from the pair is on leave.